MARKET STRUCTURE

SWING TRADING, SUPPORT AND RESISTANCE,TECHNIQUES THAT WILL TRIPPLE YOUR PROFIT

Harold Keith

TABLE OF CONTENT

INTRODUCTION

Market structure, as a thought, is the same old thing and has been around anyway extensive cash related business regions themselves. Anyway, the center rules keep on being fundamental, particularly concerning dismantling cost improvement and seeing trading cost open entrances.

Market structure goes probably as a helper for grasping vertical, diving, and sideways designs. Comparative principles can be used in a market, from stocks, possibilities, forex, and items, to mechanized assets like cryptographic types of cash or even genuine assets like land. Accepting for a moment that you're inquiring as to why market structure is so relevant or how you can use it, read on. We'll go through all of the basics in this delineation. Moreover you will learn about market structure trading,support and resistance using market structure,and how to set it up with the principles of the market,how to trade the market with esteem action and swing exchanging.

Market structure, in monetary viewpoints, suggests how various endeavors are depicted and separated thinking about their declaration and nature of dispute for work and things. Taking into account the qualities impact the way to deal with acting and outcomes of affiliations working in a particular market.

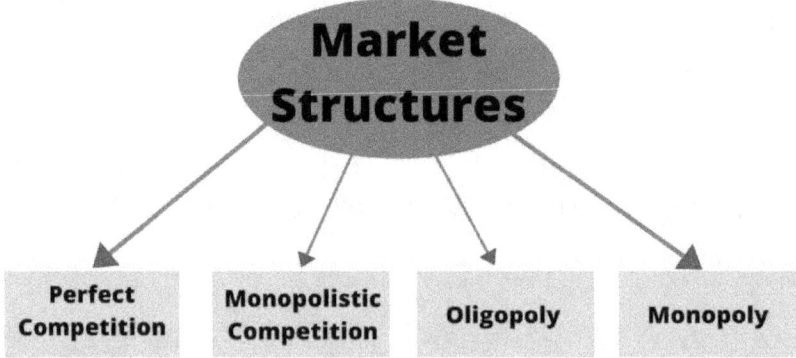

CHAPTER 1

WHAT IS MARKET STRUCTURE IN TRADING

Market structure definition: The framework or development that any given market is at present exchanging. Market development can help you with sorting out the approach to acting, condition, and current movement of the market. It highlights support and resistance levels, swing highs, and swing lows.

Types of Market structure

Market development can be completely portrayed into three specific classes: Bullish Market Development: A bullish plan is described by a movement of better potential gains (HH) and seriously encouraging depressed spots (HL). The example happen in a comparable bearing until the asset cost records a lower low (LL).

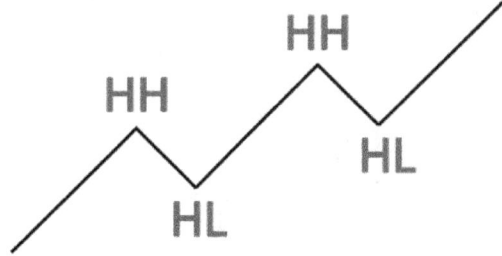

Negative Market Design: A negative development is portrayed by additional horrible discouraged spots (LL) and more unfortunate high centers (LH). The cost plan proceed to the degree that more lamentable high centers (LH) are being printed and until a higher high (HH) is made

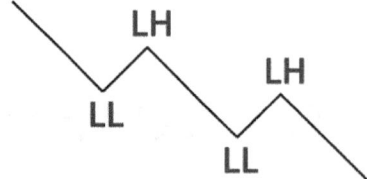

Sideways Market structure: The even improvement of cost shown by indistinguishable highs (EH) and practically identical lows (EL) is known as a sideways plan or once in a while suggested as hack.

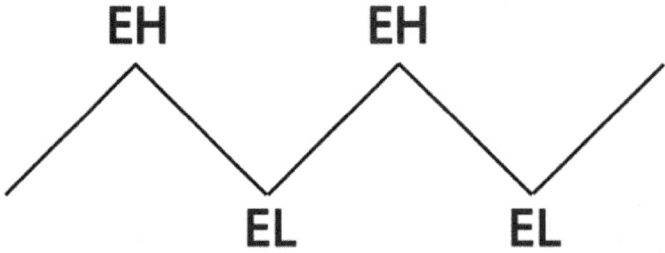

Market structure With Candles

Market development can likewise be depicted by candles as tended to under

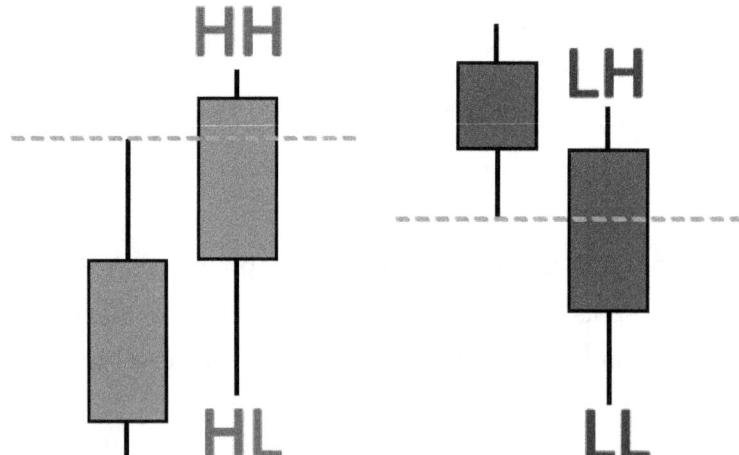

Esteem Continuation

To affirm a model it's fundamental to see candles close over the past higher high (in an ascent) or under the past lower low (in a downtrend).

This shows the continuation of purchasing as the cost increments or the continuation of selling as the cost diminishes.

Esteem Disappointment

In the event that cost activity clears over the past higher high yet, closes under, this shows shortcoming and could be the early indication of an inversion:

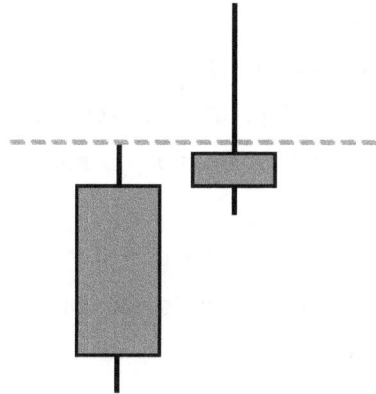

CHAPTER 2

SUPPORT AND RESISTANCE MARKET STRUCTURE

Price advancement is regularly bound inside the impediments of help and obstruction levels. Cost can cross these levels and shift to different areas of help and obstacle.

Support: An expense level that can stop a downtrend because of a centralization of interest or purchasing interest. Support levels routinely contain perpetual purchase orders in the sales book from basic market people.

Deterrent: An expense level that repulses an ascent because of the improvement of a drawn out number of merchants. Block levels contain a high volume of sell orders in the requesting book.

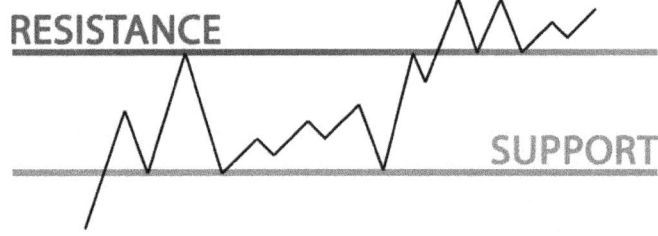

Why Is Market structure Basic in exchanging?
Market structure is tremendous for both new and able experts since it can impact the liquidity and worth activity of a market. It's also conceivably of the most
overall utilized strategies to make sense of plans, perceive potential inversion communities, and figure out current monetary conditions.

Since market structure is an impression of the two-way closeout process and mental changes of market appraisal, it gives mind blowing data into how the market is acting. It can give huge pieces of information about where the cost activity is going right away.

Market structure in addition assists with making proficient business regions (resource costs mirror each suitable datum). Market creators are a critical piece of this and supply liquidity to guarantee smooth exchanges.

Little by little rules to Utilize Market Improvement
Market improvement can assist you with depicting if conditions. For instance, in the event that an improvement break happens, want to get short on a pullback.

The Model Is Your companion
Perhaps of the most striking verbalization in the exchanging scene, and for good explanation. On the off chance that you can utilize market improvement to perceive a model, generally, the cost will occur in an equivalent course pulling out all the stops.
Force
This is an immediate consequence of the unmistakable truth that purchasers (in a bullish model) are as of now present. To change the course, serious venders should enter the market. Colossal volume should not just completed the constant power in any case to then switch the bearing.

Near as trading the heading of a quickly moving vehicle, energy is first expected to stop the vehicle (breaking). Then, more energy should begin going the substitute way (turning).

Plans

Famous trading plans like head and shoulders, backward head and shoulders, twofold bottoms, and twofold tops are fundamentally various kinds of market structures. They can address configuration breaks or model continuation.

Which Resources Work Best with Market structure?

Resources and exchanging instruments that have high liquidity, perpetual

people, and a high volume have a smoother and even more clear market structure. Forex, conceivable outcomes, securities, and stocks are plainly fit to highlight structure evaluation.

The going with business region structure model is taken from the EURUSD forex market and has an obvious bullish arrangement:

Regardless, additional unpretentious stocks and a low-cap modernized money related structures could require sufficient liquidity to shape an ideal market structure, particularly on low time intervals

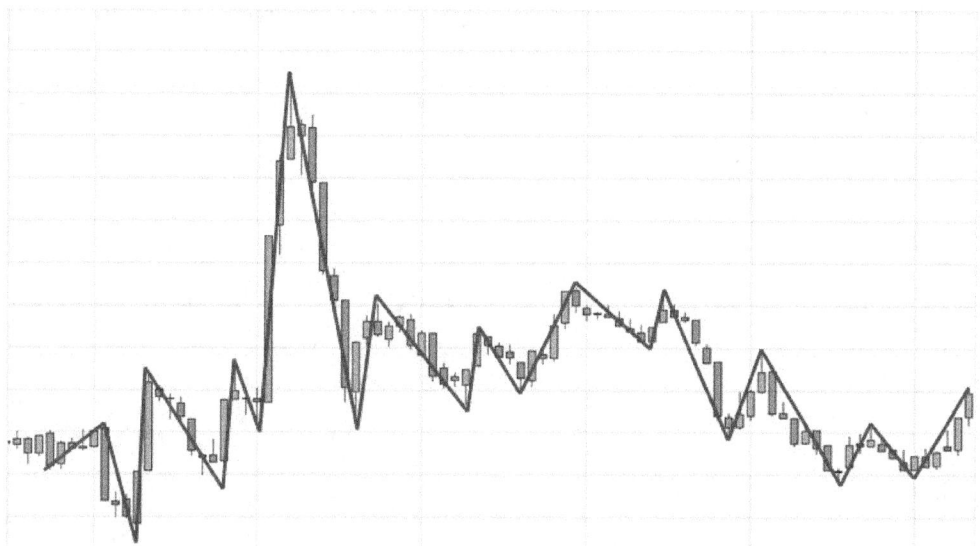

What is the Best Time span to Perceive Market structure?

Market structure shows up across all time frames and different time frames routinely show different market structures.

For instance, while the general market structure on the higher time frame might be climbing, the lower time span setup might be in a current downtrend as the market pulls back, anticipating that the mix of purchasers should go on with the higher time frame move

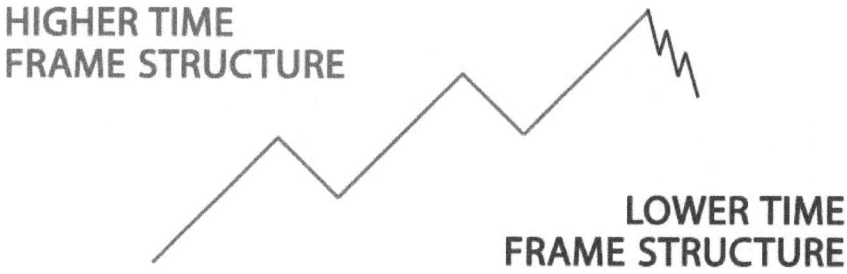

Higher volume is watched out for on higher time frames, and that proposes more market people and more solid evaluation. This general outcomes in a more reliable market structure.

On lower periods of time, the market design can frequently be more subtle and sliced from highs to lows.

The best procedure is to have a reasonable comprehension of the market overall. This unites low time frame, medium time frame, and high timeframe structure. Think about how each time frame arranges.

Time Frame	Volume	Market Structure	Trading Style
Low	Low	Testing to recognize (sever	Scalping and Day Trading
Medium	Medium	Somewhat unmistakable	Day Trading and Swing Trading
High	High	Easy to perceive	

CHAPTER 3

EXAMLPES AND TRADE SETUPS USING MARKET STRUTURE

Market structure isn't a trading philosophy or unequivocal plan. Even more an obvious level thought grants you to recognize and understand as a rule circumstances.

It might be used to help with trade segments or even more basically, set invalidation levels and know when you're misguided. You can moreover administer trades and watch using market structure principles.

Here are some market structure models:

Pullback or Retracement: When the market is in an up or downtrend, this model shows that the expense will push back and accumulate orders (making a fire the alternate way) preceding procedure with the example

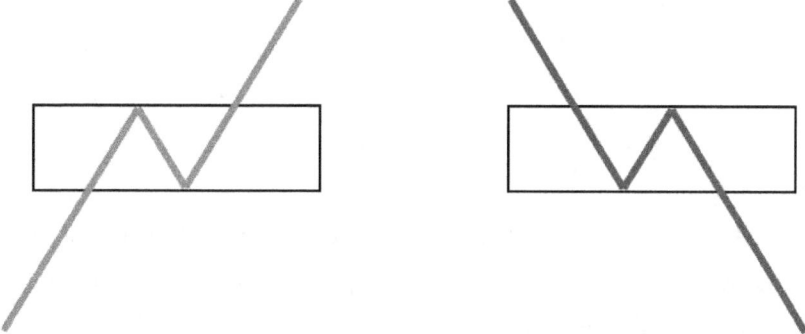

Structure Hold: This is essentially a re-appearance of a past pullback, then, the continuation of the overwhelming example. It can achieve got shippers

that guess that the market ought to pivot yet note how the example stays in a single piece. No more regrettable depressed spots (in the bullish model) or on the other hand better potential gains (in the negative model) are made.

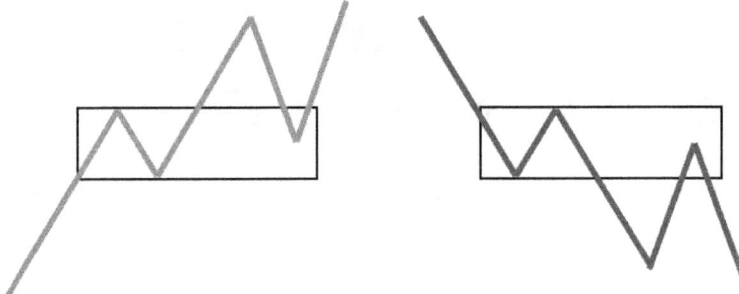

Continuation: This is a bullish or negative development where cost shapes a short cementing or base preceding pushing higher. During the base time period, agents reaccumulate or modify what is going on completely anticipating the accompanying show or drop. This can approach a triangle or banner plan.

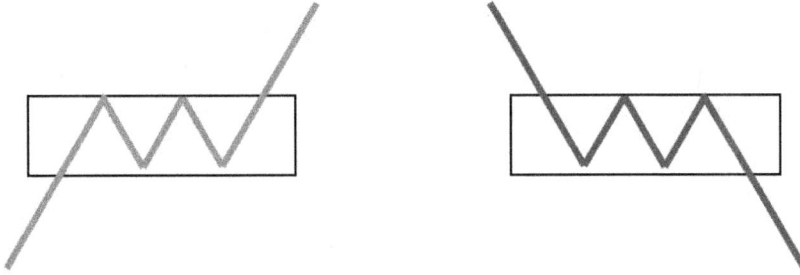

Benefits

Other than the way that market structures outfit you with a sensible blueprint of current monetary circumstances and examples, but it can similarly help you with perceiving support and resistance levels.

While using market development to find sponsorship and check, look left and endeavor to recognize districts that have been dependably respected long term. If various tests have been performed at a comparative level there is a higher open door the level will be respected from here on out

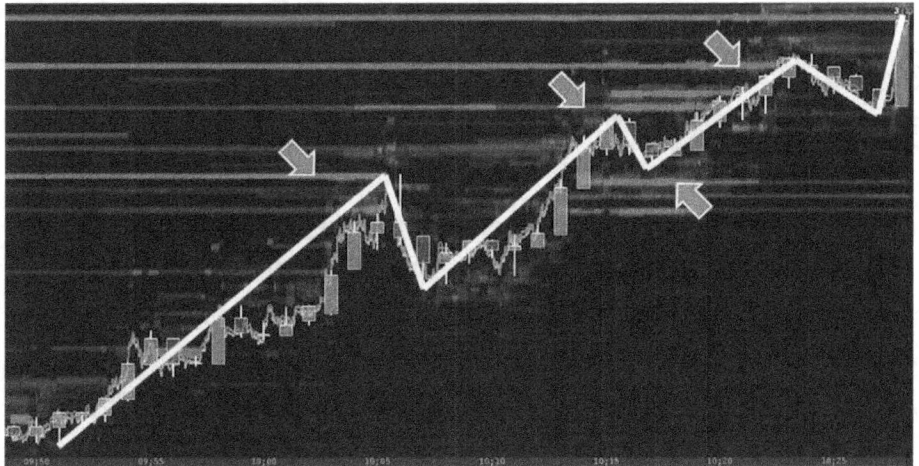

Sort out Market structure

Another benefit of using market structure in trading is that the market joins the total understanding of various individuals, loads it according to the size of the trades they make, and allows analysts to get a handle on the total assessment.

Market structure partakes in the advantage of portraying when and at what cost to exchange through pattern lines and cost objective targets, which enjoys a tremendous benefit. Resulting to choosing and looking at the lines of a likely turn of events, these limits connect with a particular expense and time works with that can be used to create express trading and hazard control methods.

Limitations

Recall that the market can do anything unexpectedly. Weakness of the market ought to be embraced and recognized. While market configuration can give hints, there are decidedly no confirmations and it simply takes one enormous powerful buyer or seller to break the example.

Market structure guidelines could appear extremely essential, but the confounded nuances can require various years to rule.

CHAPTER 4

PRINCIPLES OF MARKET STRUCTURE

1. Cost moves inside an underlying of help and obstruction.
2. A breakout of the underlying of help or obstruction will prompt cost development in the following region of the help or opposition

Price moves within a structural of support and resistance.
A breakout of the structural of support or resistance will lead to price movement in the next area of the support or resistance

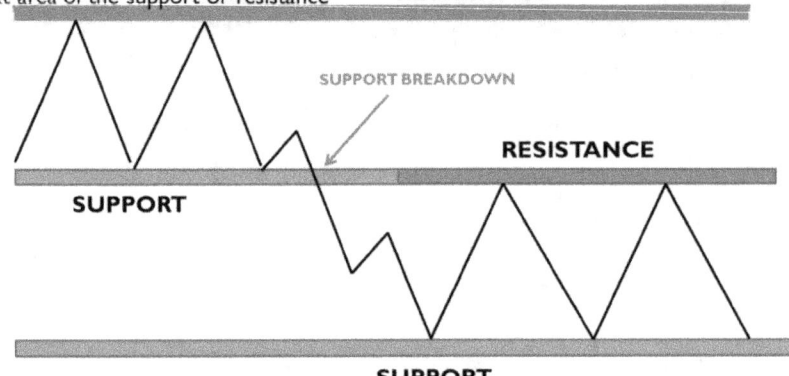

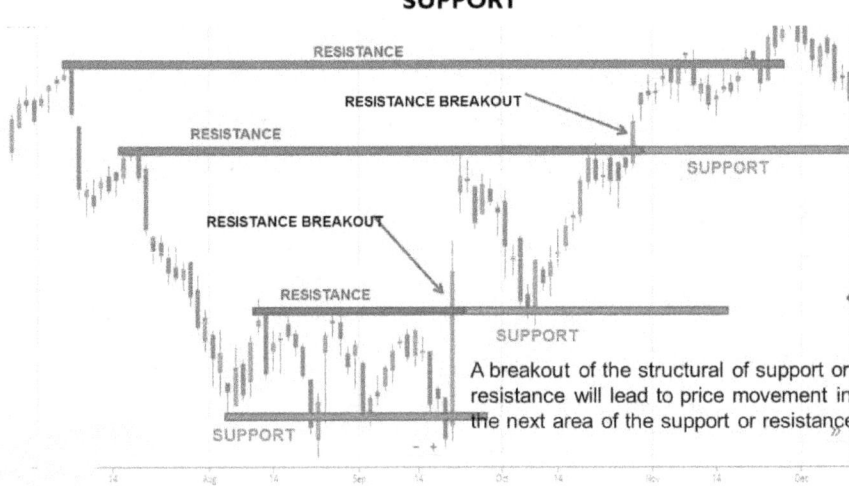

A breakout of the structural of support or resistance will lead to price movement in the next area of the support or resistance

Components of the Market structure

The market structure comprises of

2Stages

   3. Pattern

Stages

How does the market truly function?

All monetary business sectors work on the all inclusive law of Market interest.

Law of Interest The higher the cost of a thing, the less the interest (purchasers would rather not buy at a more exorbitant cost) and lower the cost, higher the interest (purchasers need to purchase at a low cost)

Law of Supply-The higher the cost of a thing, the higher the inventory (venders need to sell at a more exorbitant cost) and lower the cost, bring down the stock (dealers would rather not supply at a lower cost

So costs go up to track down venders and afterward go down to track down purchasers

We should think according to the point of view of brilliant cash

What is smart money?

Smart money are only expert cash, huge flexible investments and organization's

If you have any desire to be an effective merchant you need to comprehend where these brilliant cash put in themselves and where their requests are

In the event that you don't have a clue about this you could get caught by savvy cash

The price goes through 4 Stages

1 ACCUMULATION

2 UPTREND

3 DISTRIBUTION

Collection

- Collection implies eliminated from the drifting inventory of stock by purchasing
- Request coming in to continuously survive and retain the stock and to help the stock at this level

How smart money do that? they purchase however much of the stock as could reasonably be expected, without altogether setting the cost facing their own purchasing until there are not many, or no more offers accessible at the cost level they have been purchasing at

Gathering for the most part happens inside a clear cut clog region, where the stock seems to have no interest to one or the other drop up or drop down. The shrewd cash guarantees that the stock is contained under a specific upper level which is the inventory region. Simultaneously, the shrewd cash likewise upholds the costs over a specific lower line which is the help region.

How in all actuality does drift change?

- Halting action(stopping the downtrend)
- Change of character(strength of pattern change from negative to bullish)
- Testing of supply(testing supply regardless of whether present)
- Mark up(if no stockpile found in testing activity)

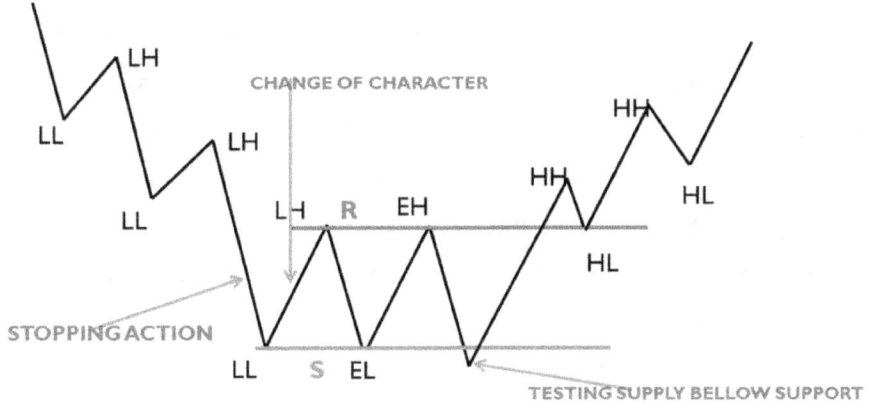

We will talk about this top to bottom in later segments. There are numerous different examples that mean aggregation. Some of them are

- adjusting bottoms,
- turn around head and shoulder and
- twofold bottoms designs
- triple base example

Upturn

When the inventory sees by smart money. At the point when general economic situations seem great, the smart money can then increase the cost

of the stock eventually

In the first place, the market breaks out from the finish of the collection stage, moving higher consistently, with normal volume. There is no rush as the insiders have purchased at discount costs and presently need to expand benefits by gathering bullish speed gradually, as the majority of the conveyance stage will be finished at the highest point of the pattern, and at the greatest costs conceivable. Once more, allowed the opportunity, we would do likewise

DISTRIBUTION

Smart money will exploit the greater costs acquired in the assembly to take benefits by starting to offer the stock back to the ignorant dealers/financial backers

Inverse of collection process

DOWNTREND

When the circulation finished. the Brilliant Cash can then write down the cost of the stock eventually. How about we consolidate all stage

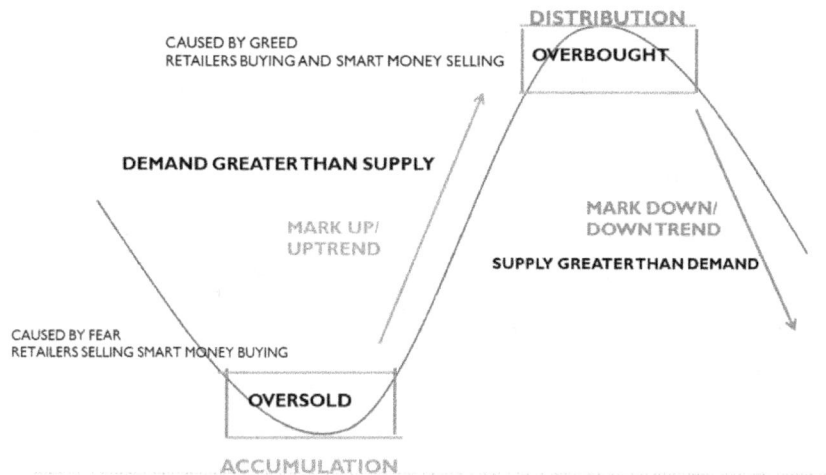

So, let's try to put the above phases

This is all the smart money is doing, they are essentially playing on the feelings of the business sectors which are driven by only two. Dread and covetousness. That is all there is to it. Make sufficient trepidation and individuals will sell. Make sufficient avarice and individuals will purchase. It's all extremely straightforward and consistent

This pattern of collection and dissemination is then rehashed unending, and across all the time periods. Some might be significant moves, and others minor, however they happen consistently and in each market

Patterns:

Allow us first to comprehend what is a pattern. In a solid bull pattern, the rise for the most part surpass the downswing long and making a higher high and higher low, the converse is valid for the bear market

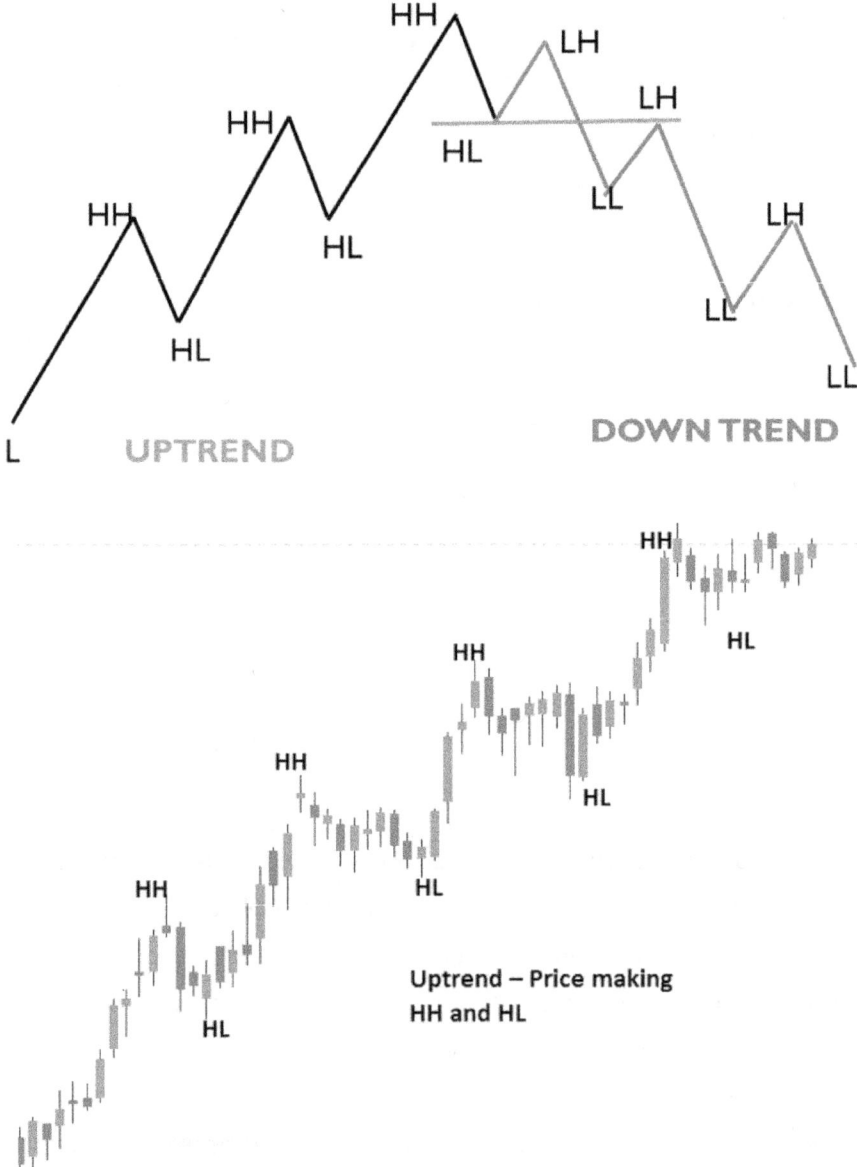

CHAPTER 5

WHY TREND ANALYSIS FOR TRADING

- ☐Exchanging against the example, without an example, or bad quality examples are potentially of the most generally perceived reason sellers misfire.
- ☐The quality or strong examples have seriously obvious accomplishment (edge)
- ☐Controlled course of action of significant worth bars and pullbacks give more noticeable sureness that pivots at natural market happen
- ☐Poor or fragile examples have lower consistency
- ☐Uncontrolled approach of significant worth bars and pullbacks into natural market diminishes chances of a reversal

Concluding the market design

As demonstrated by Dow Speculation, the market has three examples

Fundamental example: In Dow Speculation, the fundamental example is in like manner remembered to be as a huge example keeping watch. It has a long impact

Discretionary example: Dow calls a cure in the fundamental example as a helper design. In a bullish market, the discretionary example will be a slipping turn of events and in a negative market, it will be a show.

Passing example: The Minor Example is a healing move inside the discretionary example

Which time frame design is great?

- ☐It depends upon what time frame you are looking at.
- ☐Greater Time spans spread out and overpower the example.
- ☐Expecting we are looking at the everyday time span and cost is making exceptional speeds surrounding we are in the emphatically moving business sector
- ☐Regardless, if we are looking at a retracement of that bull move rapidly stretch of time we might be a transient bear market in spite of the way that general market is bullish

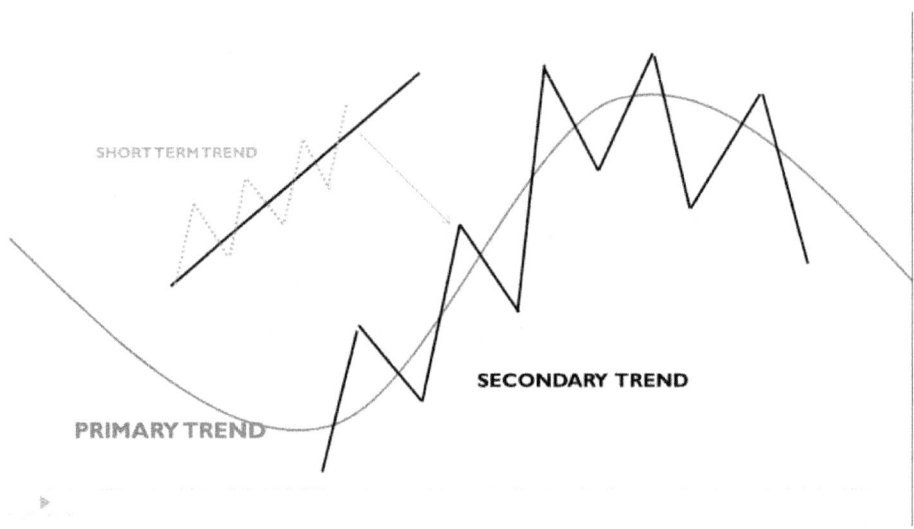

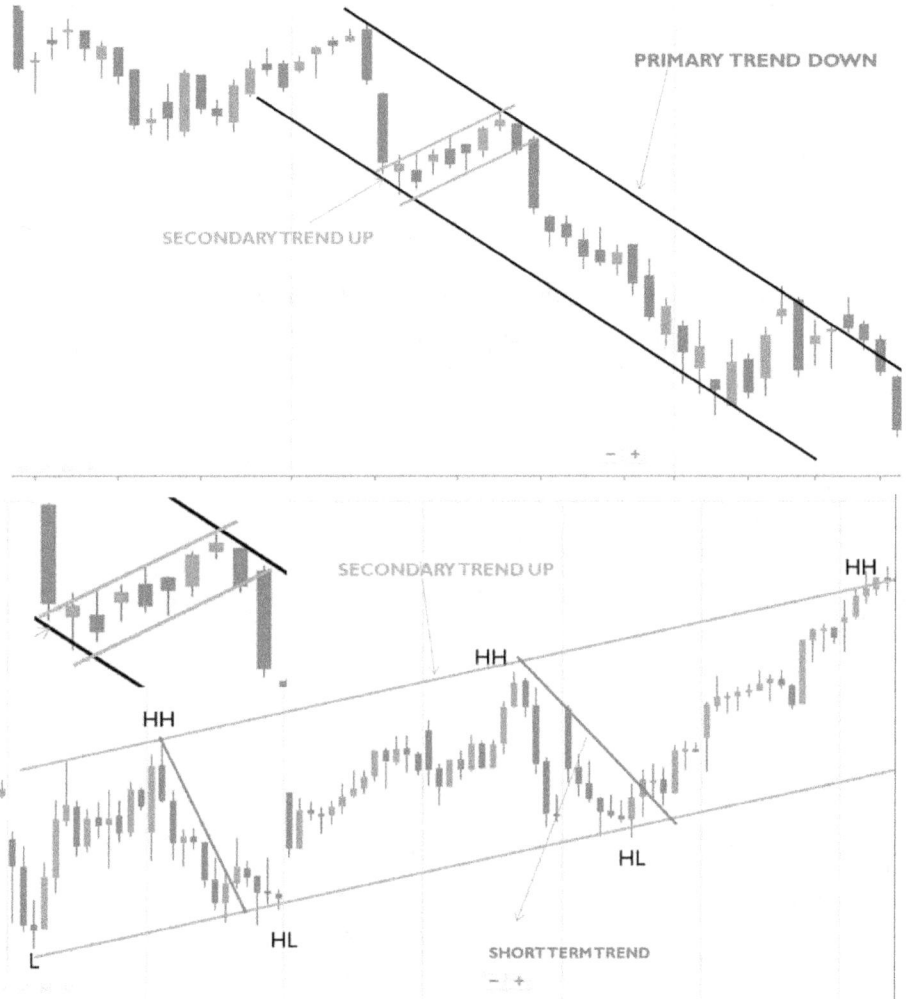

A conclusive objective of specific assessment is to find the area of example and trade as shown by the example

A piece of the instruments which are used for specific examination are

- ☐Swing(the building block of example)
- ☐Sponsorship and obstacle
- ☐market revenue zone
- ☐design line

☐

- plan
- ☐openings
- ☐volume
- ☐open interest
- ☐signal flame for area

Compassionately watch the going with video in the event that you profoundly want to learn and grasp the Market Development in Trading thought an unrivaled way

CHAPTER 6

UNDERSTANDING MARKET STRUCTURE THROUGH SWING

In this way by seeing business sector swing, we can investigate the plan of the market and get snippets of data about

1. The continuous heading of the market(trend)
2. Strength of example (exchanging pressure)
3. Backing and hindrance
4. When will the example change?
5. when to buy/sell/exit

Why Swing centers are huge?

These centers are not inconsistent, they are made by the market. They address transient changes and solicitation and supply powers. The bulls couldn't move the market over the swing high. This truly means that by then, at that point, no one had the option to offer an expense higher than the swing high. Agents saw no value over the swing high. Later on, his point could go about as deterrent.

It resembles sorting out some way to scrutinize another letter set once you grasp the characters, you can examine the words, and when you know the words you can examine the story. The essential letter to rule tells you what market development causes the improvement of a transitory high or low. If you

understand this fundamental point, the meaning of all market plans will begin to straighten out.

Portraying fire

It focuses the association between current fire high and low with past light high and low

Swing high and swing low

Principles for drawing swing high and swing low: SWING HIGH or SWING LOW Contain Least 5 BAR. The middle bar ought to be higher high and higher low than the two-proceeding with bar and the two-following bar

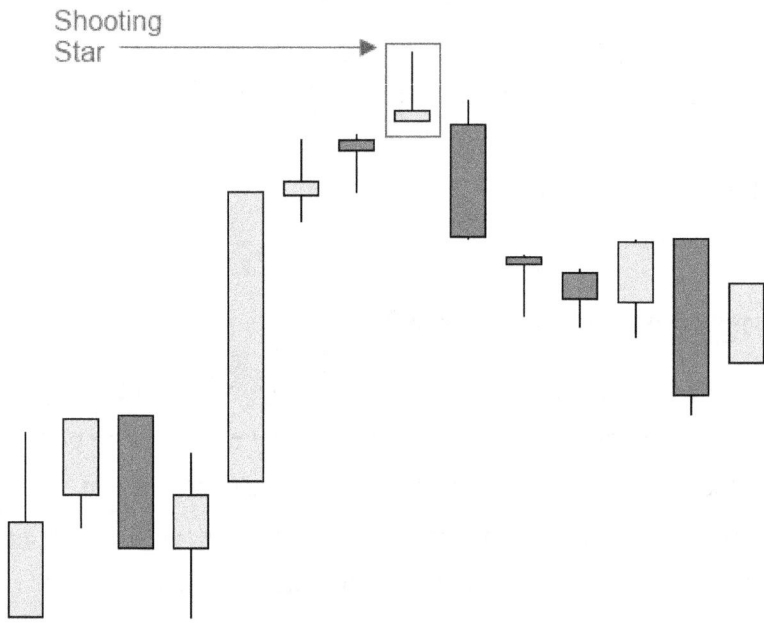

Shooting Star

Swing Types

There are two kinds of swing

- High and low
- ☐Swing high and swing low

Permit me to explain for you

Swing low (SL)

The market endeavored to drop down. Then, it stopped and the bullish example proceeded. The market broke all resistance (swing high) and made a new trend high. In that capacity, the market tumbled appallingly in its undertaking to drop down. Indisputably the base it pushed to is called swing low

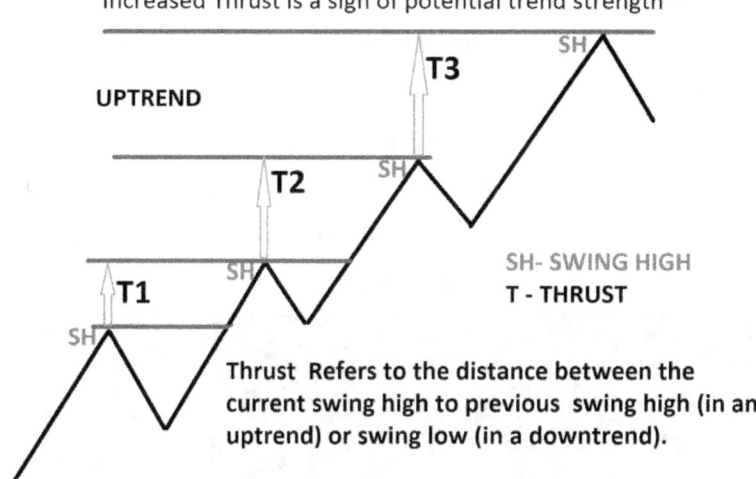

Increased Thrust is a sign of potential trend strength

UPTREND

T3

T2 SH

T1 SH

SH

SH- SWING HIGH

T - THRUST

Thrust Refers to the distance between the current swing high to previous swing high (in an uptrend) or swing low (in a downtrend).

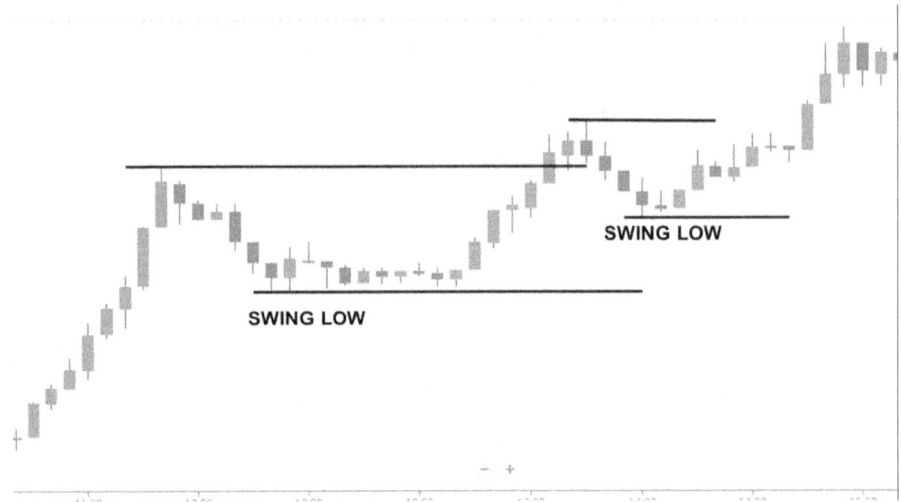

Swing interminably discouraged spot

Each critical market has some pullback that is shallow and some continue onward for one swing. Where pullback goes further and happens for more than one swing, molding a LOW. Eventually, this more significant pullback finished and the example proceeded. A low transforms into a swing low once the expense breaks out over the last silly expense high for the resumption of the bullish example. Permit me to explain for you

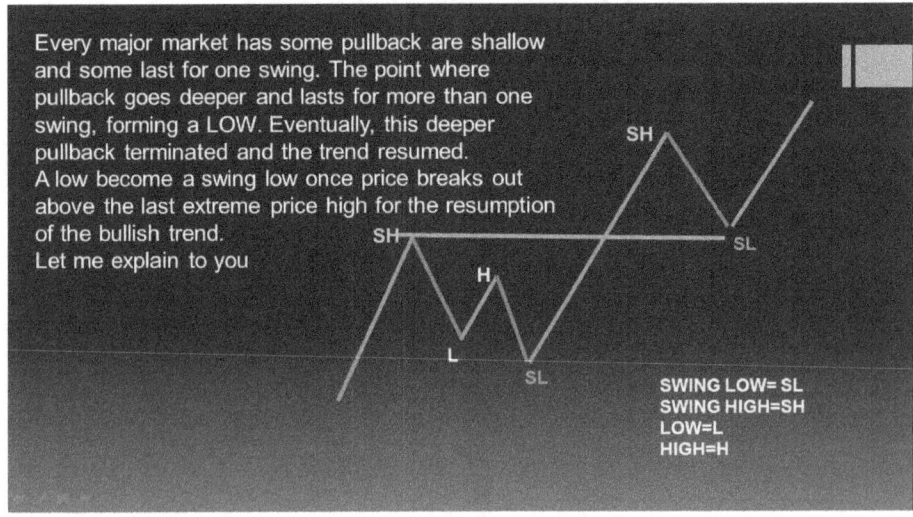

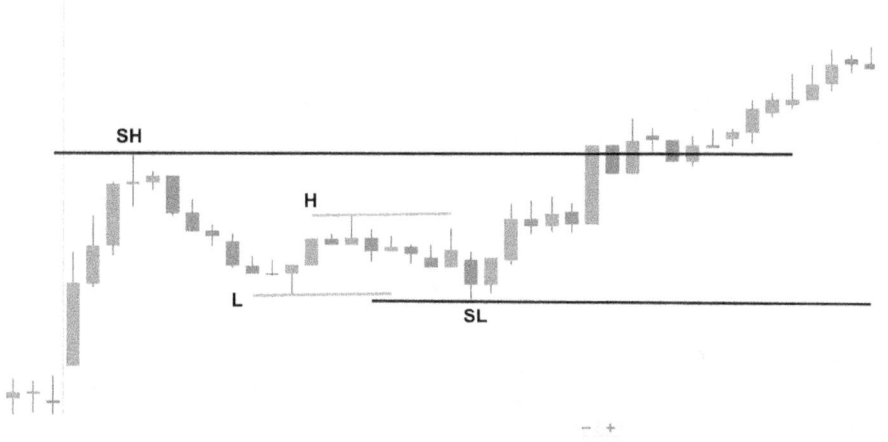

LET'S DO SOME EXAMPLE

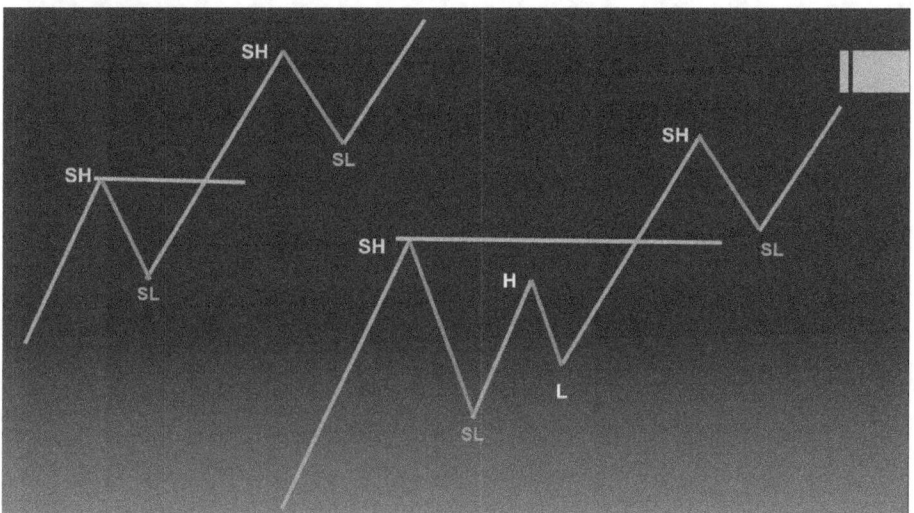

All of the thoughts inspected above are material for a swing high and high

Bit by bit guidelines to KNOW WHEN LOW BECOMES SWING LOW

Right when the expense cleared the above swing unquestionable level. To clear an expense level, the market ought to shape a light that is absolutely over the expense level. This infers if a fire low is higher than an expense level, the market has cleared over the expense level.

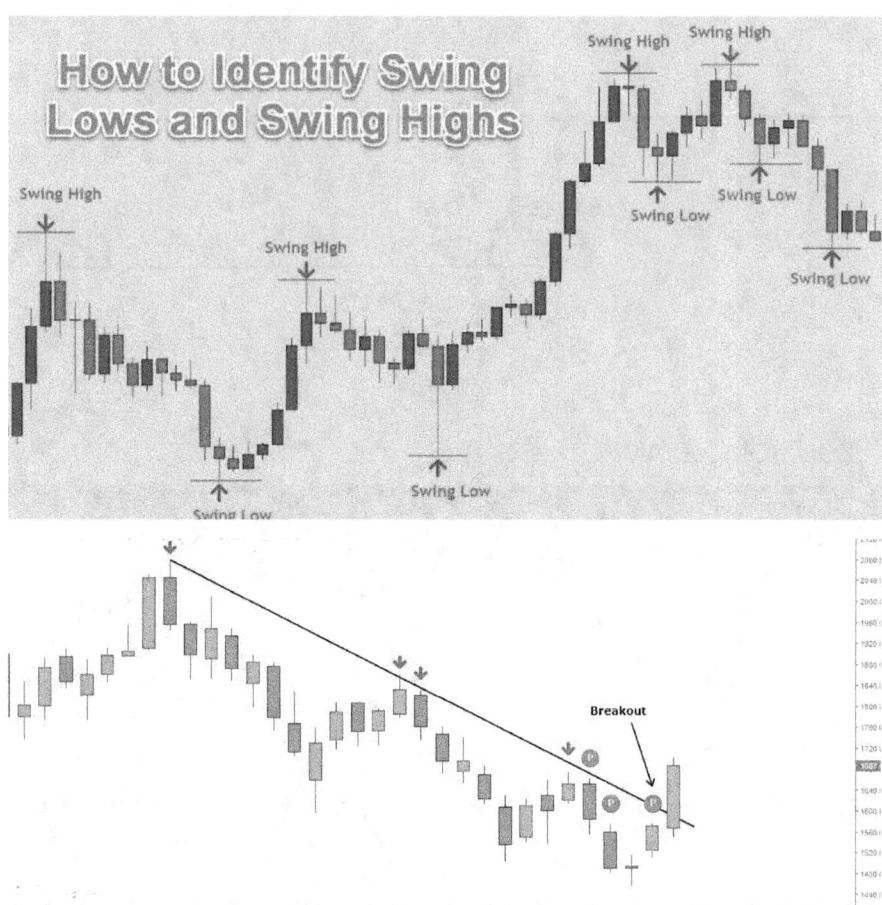

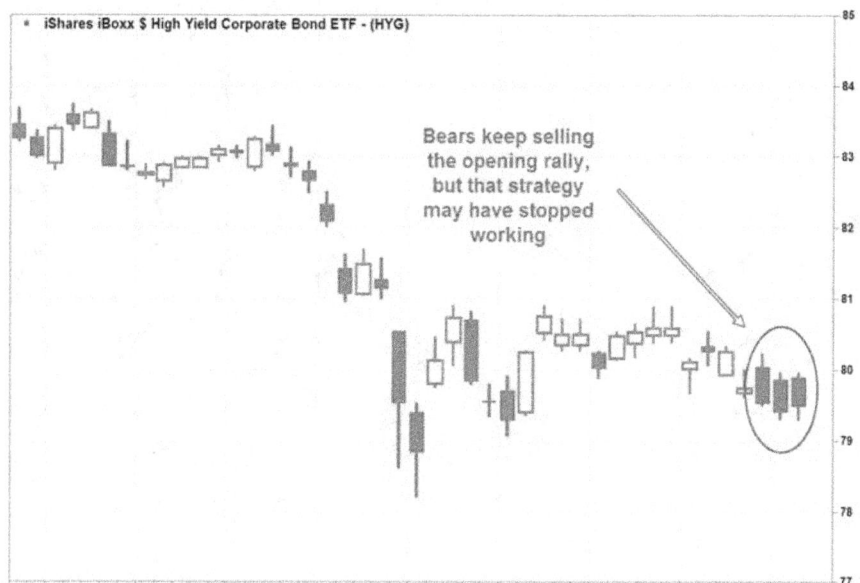

We will cover this in more detail in the expense movement point

Graph scrutinizing the swing

Graphs have authentic worth in choosing the position (region) and conceivable example of stocks, by measuring the association of natural market swing. To focus on charts, look for the expectations behind the movement which the outline shows.

Whenever you read a chart, consider what you consider there to be a proclamation of the powers that standard the expense and when the power lift from costs. Concentrate

on your chart according to the viewpoint of the approach to acting of the stock, the perspectives of individuals who are prevalent in it, and the victories and frustrations of the buyers and merchants as they fight to overpower each other

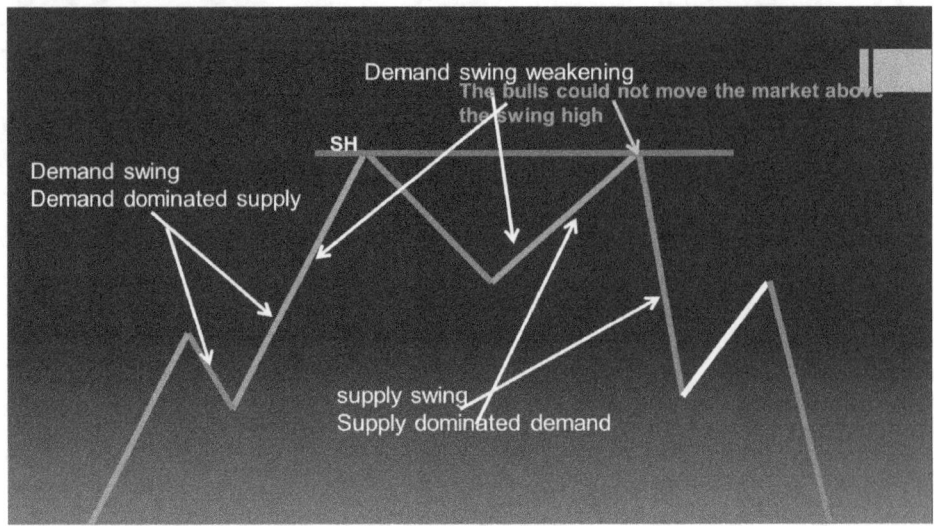

Huge real factors that impact the swing are:

1.cost turn of events

2.volume

3.The associations between esteem advancement and volume

4.The time expected for all the swing advancements

Esteem advancement and swing

Cost advancement (cost changes starting with one swing then onto the next)

Seeing the gathering of an expense swing, we can investigate the

development of the market and get signs about

sponsorship and resistance

- ☐Lines of supply and support(trend)
- ☐Changes in inspiration and reaction advancement (net expansion or

setback)

- ☐Close to strength and weakness(momentum)
- ☐Improvement of accumulating or dispersal

Swing and Support Resistance

This swing centers are not inconsistent, they are made by the market. They address transient changes and solicitation and supply powers. The bulls couldn't move the market over the swing high. This plans that by then, at that point, no one was prepared to offer an expense higher than the swing high. Sellers saw no value over the swing high.

In this way, subsequently, when the expense moves close or move toward over a swing high, we ought to recall that specialists saw no value in buying over that point in advance. Expecting that most traders have not changed their perspectives, the expense is presumably not going to move over the swing high. Effectively the swing passing mark an expense locale that goes against the market from climbing this is what we call a resistance district. Pivot for help locale

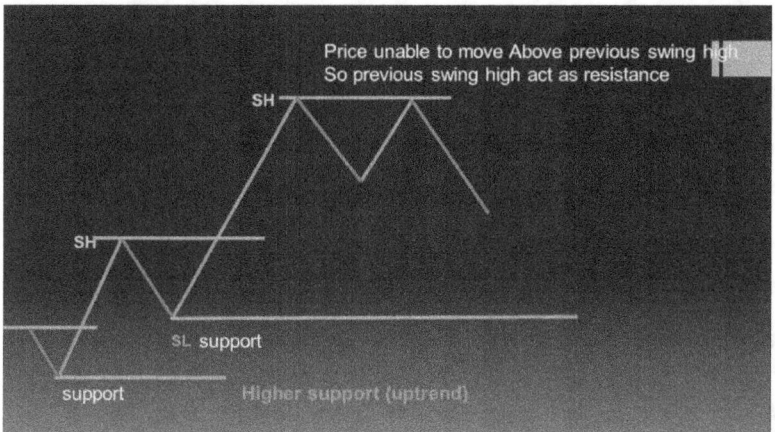

Changes in inspiration and reaction advancement (net expansion or deficiency)

By differentiating inspiration swing and recall swing we might we anytime at some point can evaluate the strength of an example

- ☐ Extended Drive swing means that potential example strength as the increment is positive. Shortening of inspiration swing means that potential example deficiency.
- ☐ The extended reaction means that the conceivable inadequacy of an example. The reduced reaction means that the probable strength of an example

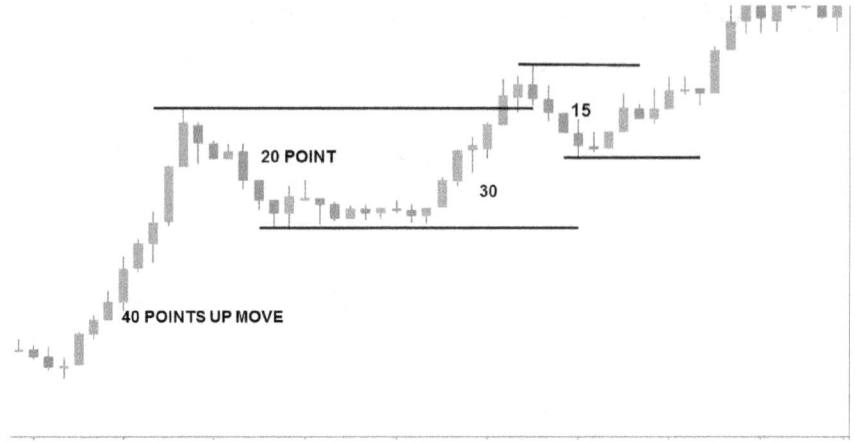

For extra nuances, assuming no one cares either way, read the going with Push Pullback article

Push Pullback

Close to strength and deficiency

- ☐Ponder the energy of the continuous expense swing with the power of the past expense swing in a comparative course.
- ☐Ponder the energy of the continuous expense swing with the power of the past expense swing the alternate way.
- ☐Is the continuous expense accelerating or decelerating? What's the
- importance here?

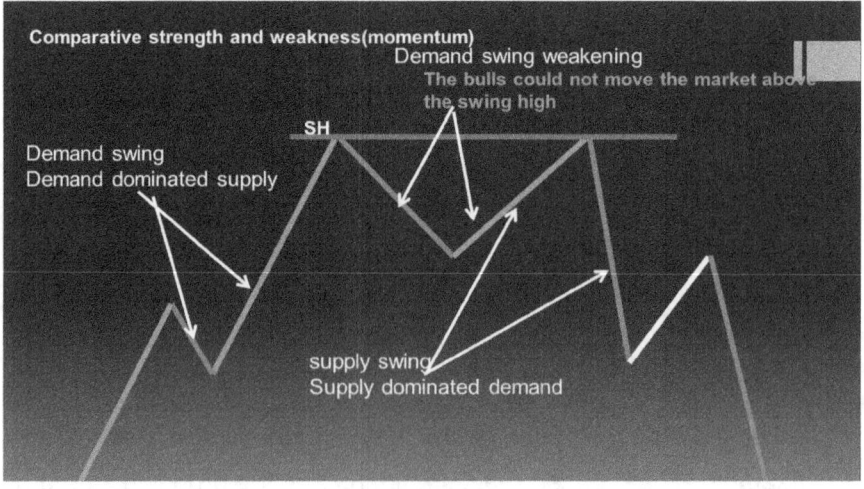

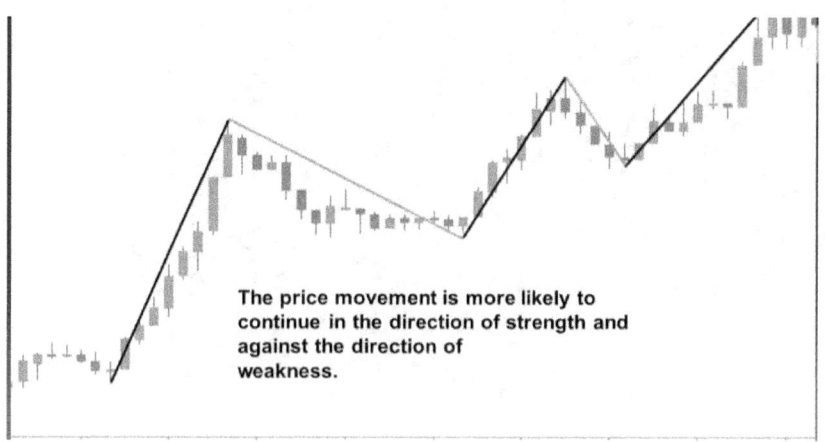

The price movement is more likely to continue in the direction of strength and against the direction of weakness.

For extra nuances, mercifully read the going with Significant level Worth Movement Examination article

Significant level Worth Movement Examination
Improvement of gathering or scattering

- ☐The dealer will buy powerfully close by as of late settled market support centers, as he is convinced that a gathering will deliver satisfactorily.

- ☐Whenever the vendor notes diminishing interest in the congregations from each help point, he sees that his opportunity for productive speculation on the 'Bull' side is in like manner diminishing

- ☐Ultimately, a gainful entryway on the long side is gone, and the master switches what is happening. Transforming into a short vendor at show tops forms the stock of stock and this augmentation builds the propelling imbalance hanging toward the sellers over the buyers. Again, the advancement to an example condition is accomplished with the line of least resistance presently being a negative one

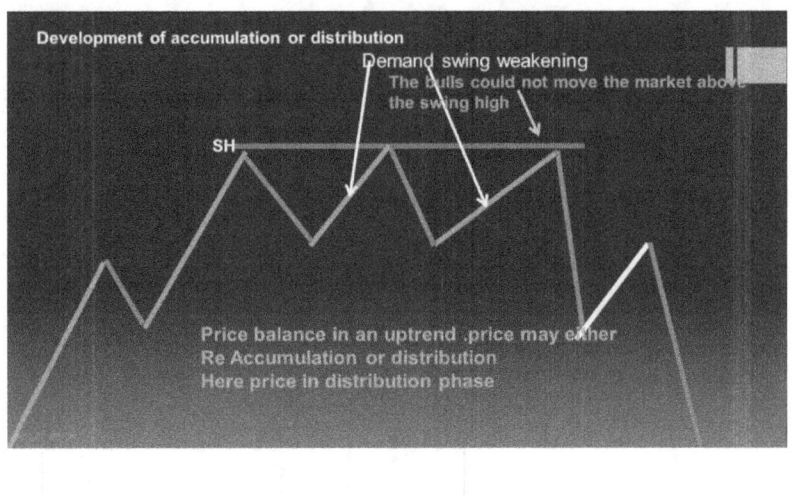

Model and swing

Might we at some point join the above factors as a whole. Standard explicit appraisal says the market drops in the up-down wave, what we call market swing. In a sound bull plan, the climb for the most part outflanks the downswing long, the inverse is significant for the bear market. Right when a model neglects to make another high (blockaded rally), it perhaps shows a model change (sideways or inversion).

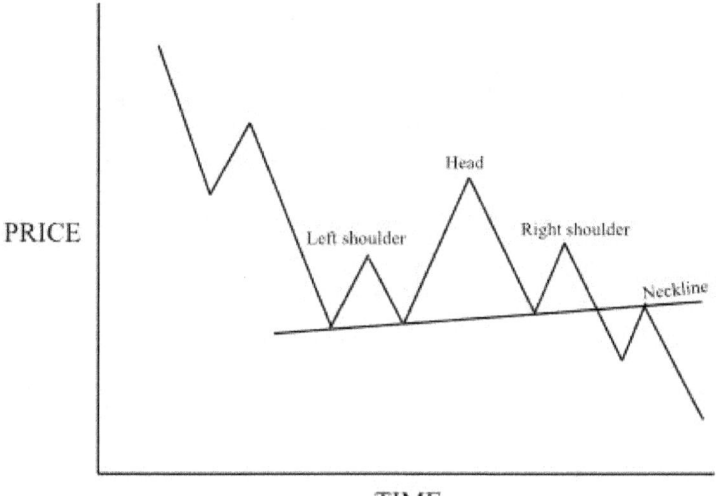

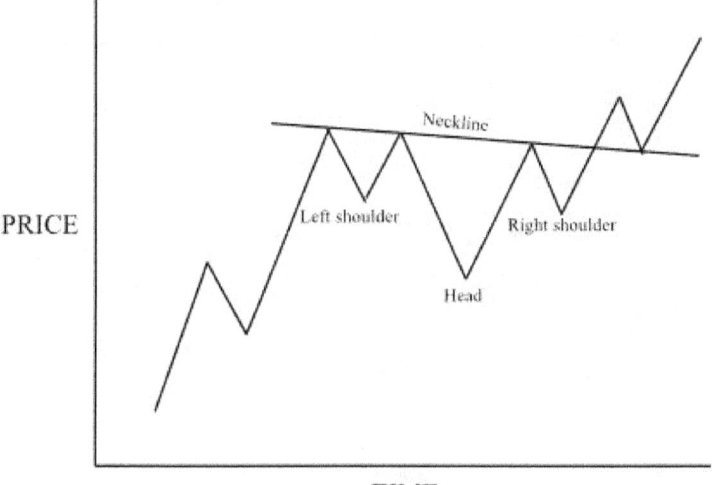

Volume exchanged each swing

- Volume (when to purchase/sell/exit) of exchanging on elective trading waves
- ☐Broadening or diminishing the kind of market income
- ☐☐Trading top
- ☐☐Movement or force of exchanging (the restriction of bull and bear to draw in following on advances and decline. rallies and response
- ☐☐Attributes of market income whether fundamental, theoretical, or solid

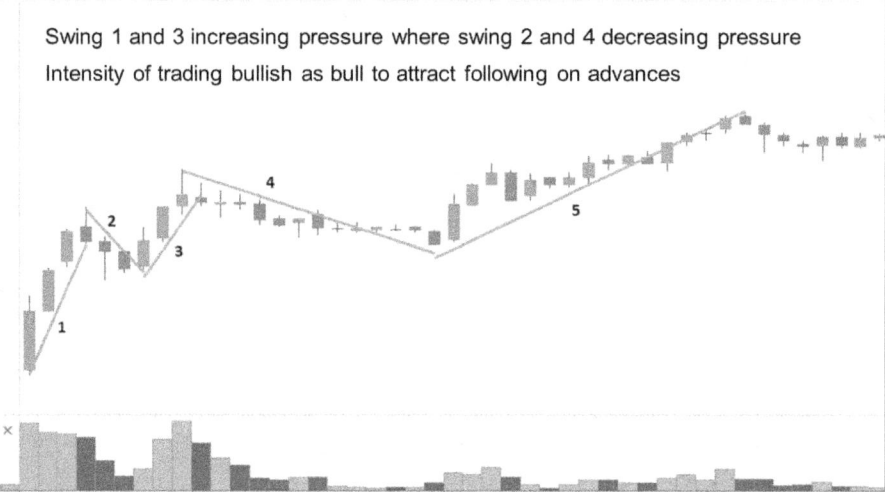

Swing 1 and 3 increasing pressure where swing 2 and 4 decreasing pressure
Intensity of trading bullish as bull to attract following on advances

For additional subtleties, accepting nobody minds one way or the other, read the going with Volume Worth Development Assessment article

Volume Worth Activity

Volume and cost of each swing

Volume and cost progression give the best associate in:

1. Deciding the heading of coming moves.

2. Choosing when to trade.

3. Knowing when a stock is on the affiliation

4. Knowing when a move is wrapping up.

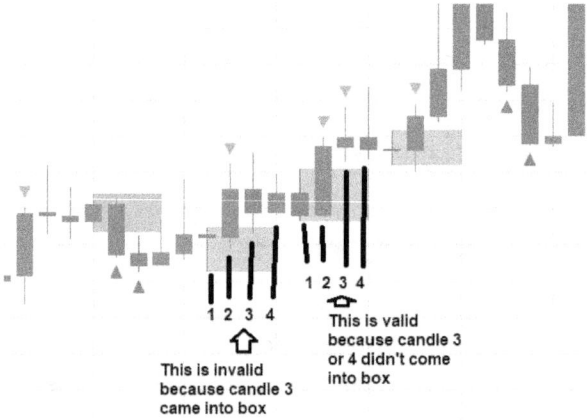

1 2 3 4
This is invalid because candle 3 came into box

1 2 3 4
This is valid because candle 3 or 4 didn't come into box

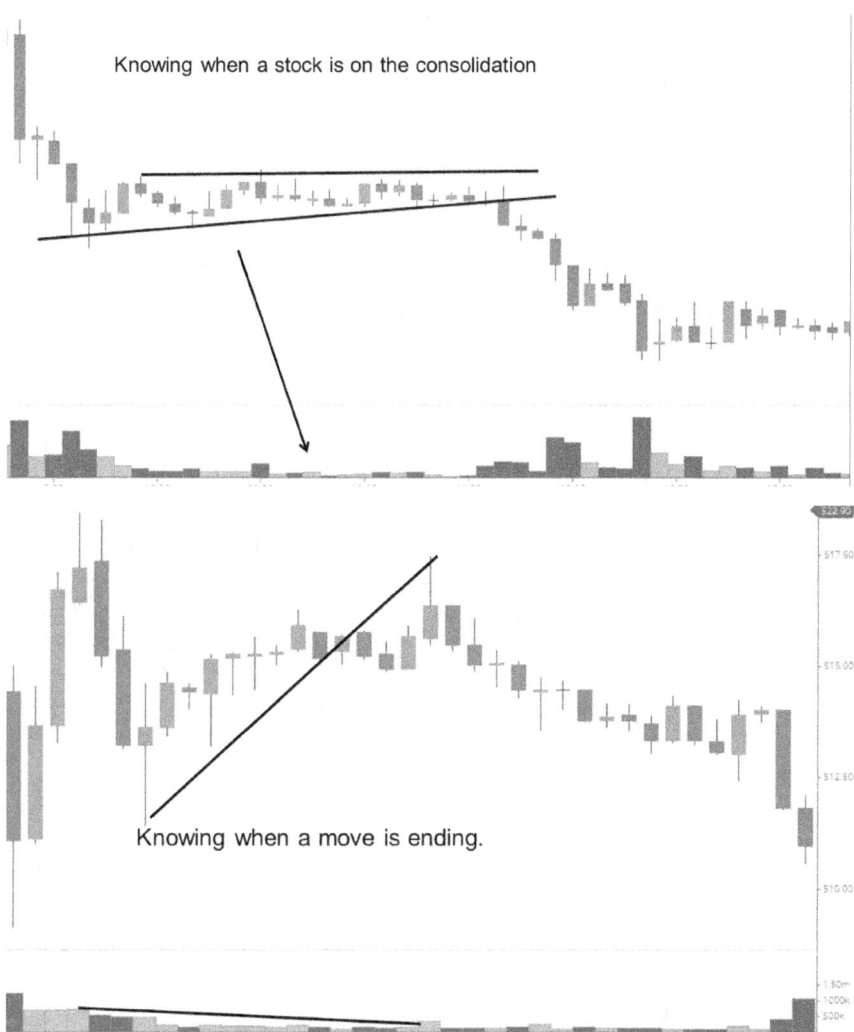

Knowing when a stock is on the consolidation

Knowing when a move is ending.

Advancing System as opposed to Advancing Arrangement

A displaying framework depicts how a business will accomplish a particular goal or mission. This consolidates which campaigns, content, channels, and exhibiting programming they'll use to execute that mission and track its success.

For example, while a more imperative plan or office could manage electronic diversion advancing, you ought to genuinely consider your work on Facebook as a solitary displaying framework.

An advancing arrangement contains something like one exhibiting procedures. It is the design from which your displaying strategies are undeniably made and helps you with communicating each technique back to a greater advancing movement and business objective.

For example, your association is shipping off another item thing, and it accepts clients ought to join. This requires the elevating office to cultivate a

displaying plan that will help with familiarizing this thing with the business and drive the ideal data trades

An elevating plan should include: The continuous position, needs, and heading of your affiliation. Its circumstance relating to outside normal factors. A fundamental assessment of your affiliation's resources, inadequacies, open entryways, and risks.

www.ingramcontent.com/pod-product-compliance
Lightning Source LLC
Chambersburg PA
CBHW072237230526
45466CB00024B/2096